PRAISE FOR THE 180° CHRISTIAN

I don't know of any subject that is more pertinent and relevant to the moment in which we live. It is something that, as true Christians, we observe in our daily lives as we witness the way our culture has influenced the Church. This work is certainly timely and of benefit to any Christian who wants to walk the biblical way. I have known Pastor Conlon for many years, and he lives this life as well as the church he shepherds. His life and devotion to God attest to the fact that the subject matter he's dealing with is relevant for our times. I highly recommend the reading of this great work.

L. John Bueno
Executive Director (Ret.), Assemblies of God World Missions

I have had the opportunity to hear Pastor Carter Conlon speak on a few different occasions, and each time I was impressed at how he was always able to bring the message home to the people. He was discipled by my dear friend and spiritual father, David Wilkerson. I am just so thankful for the legacy of strong Bible-based preaching and ministry that Pastor Carter brings to Times Square Church.

Nicky Cruz
Nicky Cruz Outreach

I have great respect for Pastor Conlon and have countless times been blessed by God's work through him.

Beth Moore
Living Proof Ministries

Pastor Carter Conlon is a true man of God who lives what he preaches. He has been given a special anointing of the Holy Spirit to deliver the Word of God with straightforwardness and authority, yet with mercy and grace. When this man preaches, you know you have truly heard from God's throne.

David Wilkerson
World Challenge

Here is a book that truly speaks to the condition of the Church in America. We have much in common with the first-century church in the city of Corinth. We have succumbed to compromise, division and materialistic excess. But in these pages Pastor Carter Conlon does far more than diagnose the malady; he provides a gospel remedy—turning fully toward Jesus. I believe what we read here will turn our hearts to our first love.

Gary Wilkerson
President, World Challenge
Lead Pastor, The Springs Church

I have known Carter Conlon for many years and have witnessed his fervent heart for Christ, his love for the alienated and the poor, and his uncompromising attention to God's Word. You may not feel comfortable with everything he says, but he will force you to think and take your calling seriously.

Dr. Ravi Zacharias
Author and Speaker

THE 180° CHRISTIAN

CARTER
CONLON

THE 180°

SERVING
JESUS IN A
CULTURE OF
EXCESS

CHRISTIAN

Regal

From Gospel Light
Ventura, California, U.S.A.

From Gospel Light
Ventura, California, U.S.A.
www.regalbooks.com
Printed in the U.S.A.

Library of Congress Cataloging-in-Publication Data
Conlon, Carter.
The 180 degree Christian : serving Jesus in a culture of excess / Carter
Conlon.
p. cm.
ISBN 978-0-8307-6095-4 (hard cover)
ISBN 978-0-8307-6371-9 (trade paper)
1. Bible. N.T. Corinthians, 1st—Criticism, interpretation, etc. 2. Church—
Biblical teaching. 3. Christian life—Biblical teaching. I. Title.
BS2675.52.C66 2012
227'.206—dc23
2011035477

Rights for publishing this book outside the U.S.A. or in non-English languages are administered by Gospel Light Worldwide, an international not-
for-profit ministry. For additional information, please visit www.glww.org,
email info@glww.org, or write to Gospel Light Worldwide, 1957 Eastman
Avenue, Ventura, CA 93003, U.S.A.

To order copies of this book and other Regal products in bulk quantities,
please contact us at 1-800-446-7735.

*To all of the precious believers in Christ who have held
to biblical faith and practice in these times. God has heard
every sigh of your hearts as you have watched some of professing
Christianity drift into powerlessness. Your love of truth
will keep you safely in His arms.*

And to Teresa, the love of my life and wife of my youth.

Contents

Foreword

For some years now, believers in Jesus Christ have been forced to face a sad fact: Christianity is on the decline across America. Almost all surveys conducted by Christian pollsters reveal disturbing downward trends as they check the vital signs of Christian churches, the clergy and professing believers. Nationally, average church attendance is decreasing, as is volunteerism to serve others. Hundreds of pastors are leaving the ministry every month, and few who begin as pastors make it to retirement still in the ministry.

Several surveys now confirm what many have suspected: the lifestyles of men and women regularly attending evangelical churches are almost indistinguishable from nonbelievers, as evidenced in their priorities and value judgments. Bible study is less and less part of the normal Christian life. Instead of the Church evangelizing the world, the world and its influence have made deep inroads into Christ's Church. In addition, and not surprisingly, some of the largest evangelical denominations have experienced negative growth over the past decade.

In some places, thankfully, signs of God's grace abound. There *are* churches that are effectively spreading the gospel and growing numerically. There *are* many believers who are still clinging to the eternal truths of God's Word and confessing Jesus Christ unashamedly. But any objective analysis of the big spiritual picture must result in some sobering conclusions: the Christian Church faces radical challenges and problems as we move through the early decades of the twenty-first century.

Radical problems often require radical solutions. In *The 180° Christian*, Carter Conlon, who pastors Times Square Church in New York City and travels widely around the world, presents a powerful answer to the current decline of Christianity in our nation, our churches, and even in our own lives. He masterfully analyzes the core spiritual problems that bog us down and shows the way out so we can return to God's will and blessing on our lives. He makes a clear and convincing case for the need of a 180° turn back to God.

If you tend toward accepting a shallow spiritual lifestyle, this book will make you feel uncomfortable. But if you're hungry for more of Jesus, it will feed your soul and impart fresh inspiration.

Jim Cymbala
Senior Pastor, The Brooklyn Tabernacle

Preface

The last word had been preached and the last song had been sung, yet nobody moved. Our Sunday afternoon worship service was over, but it wasn't at all.

Without warning, an overwhelming presence of God moved through our church. Hundreds of people stayed and prayed. Some fell to their knees, others sat almost motionless straight through to the next service.

At that evening's gathering an even more unusual thing happened: Silence. The choir was assembled on stage, but no one was singing the usual praises. Instead, a solemn hush fell over the entire sanctuary. At that point, everyone at Times Square Church, New York City, knew that things would not be going as planned. We put aside every agenda that night other than to seek the face of God.

During that season, we felt led of God to cancel all church events—our upcoming missions conference, guest speaker appearances, every ministry activity. The Lord was clearly calling us to pray. In fact, months prior, as one of our associate pastors and I were traveling back to the city from upstate New York, I was reading aloud from the book of Hebrews as he drove. The more I read, the more both of us were gripped with an urgency to study this book as a congregation, particularly Hebrews 4:16, which admonishes us to "come boldly unto the throne of grace, that we may obtain mercy, and find grace to help in time of need." We knew it was a mercy call. Something was coming, and God was preparing us so that *we* as a church might be of help in time of need.

For weeks this unusual manifestation of God's presence permeated our services. Although the eyes of the congregation would look to us for direction, there were times when we as pastors could only kneel before the Lord. It was as if God were saying, "No flesh will lead this." Some moments were marked by a great cry for mercy sounding from the entire congregation. Other times that same holy silence would fall over the sanctuary—leaving us with no choice but to linger in God's presence. Pastor David Wilkerson, the founder of our church, simply concluded, "God has called a solemn assembly."

In the thickness of God's presence, we could not help but examine every part of our hearts. It was a time of deep conviction, of allowing God to cleanse and prepare us to go forward in unity. There came an utter awareness that no thing was a light thing, and these were by no means light times. We instinctively knew that the Lord was warning us of an impending calamity that would come to our city—a time of shaking. At the same time, God repeatedly assured us that He was in control and that we were not to be fearful—we were to be full of the Holy Spirit. We were to be the Body of Christ with arms open, ready to receive those who would be caught unawares.

These meetings marked by God's profound presence, the holy silence, the words of warning and the burden to pray came during the summer of 2001. Although God was clearly preparing us so that we as a congregation would not be shaken, I cannot say that we knew exactly how this calamity would manifest.

On September 11, we knew.

Moments after the airplane hit the second of the Twin Towers, I walked into Times Square Church and found a few dozen people on their knees, praying and weeping. One might assume that my role as pastor at that moment would be to offer words of comfort and consolation, perhaps even to cry alongside them.

I simply clapped my hands and said, "Everyone up! We have been trained, warned and prepared for this moment. We have prayed for weeks, and now it's time to work."

Everyone got up. Within minutes we had dispatched people to buy water, food and blankets. Others assembled to start making sandwiches. One team loaded a truck and headed downtown to the World Trade Center site. How this mere church food truck was able to slip amongst a military convoy, pass through every single security checkpoint all the way down to Chambers Street, and then be permitted to park as close to the disaster site as possible could only have been the hand of God. He had prepared us, and He was going to use us. We set up a table and began 24-hour distribution of water and sandwiches to first responders for the first couple of weeks after the disaster.

Back on 51st and Broadway, where our church is located, we became a hub for the distribution of donated goods from not only our own congregants but also from other organizations and ministries across the United States. And our doors were open wide to receive those who came looking for a place of refuge. In they came by the hundreds—terrified, confused, lost and hungry. Not only did we offer food and a place to sleep, we also extended comfort and counsel. Many had stepped into church for perhaps the first time in their lives—having once been among the scornful, cold, and cynical. God gave us an incredible measure of grace and strength to embrace all those who continued to come in during the weeks that followed.

God's grace was apparent in other ways, too. I vividly recall attending a meeting months prior with more than a hundred business leaders—predominantly executives from the financial services community. Our intention at that meeting was to collect an offering for humanitarian aid to various countries. Instead, I was unexpectedly prompted in my spirit to take a different course. I got up and began to speak to these business executives about a debt we all owe that we can never repay ourselves. I talked about the accumulation of worldly wealth, yet the glaring absence of any security from that wealth when we die. Then I clearly stated, "This is what you must do," and I laid out the plan of God for salvation through Jesus Christ.

Sometime later, I was told that 17 of the people in that room were in the towers on the morning of 9/11. Many escaped, but some were killed.

I can only imagine what those who lost their lives must have been thinking in that last hour, knowing that death was imminent. Did they remember what the Lord had so clearly laid before them? Did they heed the warning they were graciously given?

We would be wise to take notice of a certain pattern that never fails throughout history. In the Old and New Testaments, we see time and again that the Lord is absolutely faithful to warn and prepare His people before any impending judgment or calamity. He sets His watchmen on the walls, His shepherds over the flock. When those on the watchtower see something on the horizon, it is their call of duty to sound the alarm. From that point, the people have a choice. They can heed the warning and immediately begin making preparations during the period of grace that the Lord has handed them, to the end that they will be found lacking nothing on the day it transpires—or they can disregard the warning, mocking and ridiculing the messenger, only to later find themselves besieged. Unfortunately, we see in the Scriptures that it is more often the case of the latter.

When the towers came down, although we were in no way immune to the underlying sense of horror and grief at the tragedy of it all, we as a church could not help but stand in awe of the mercy and faithfulness of God. We recognized that we had been prepared—as if the Lord had allowed us our time to grieve before the towers fell so that we would be ready when He needed us to be there for others. Interestingly, several choir members who worked in the towers later testified to being uncharacteristically late for work that morning due to various reasons. Another congregant was released from her job shortly before that day without explanation. One of our pastor's sons who had an interview scheduled for 10 A.M. that morning in the North Tower instead found himself at home, watching incredulously as the events unfolded. He had initially tried to get an earlier time slot but was unable to.

Of course, I am not suggesting that all of God's people will always be spared in a calamity, for we know this is simply not true. Yet in this particular instance, for the sake of God's purposes, we were. We had heeded His warnings, and God had prepared and protected us.

And now, I sense a stirring in my heart again.

In like measure, I feel that some very, very difficult days are just ahead of us. And just as the Lord prepared a church in the middle of Times Square before the events of 9/11 hit New York City, I believe we are living in an hour when God, in His mercy, is preparing His Church at large. Times of immense hardship will hit this Church age, and whether it will be experienced collectively or individually, we are all destined to go through the fire. Everything that can be shaken will be shaken, and only what was born and sustained by truth will remain. You and I must be prepared again. Now our job is not to be concerned with the times or the hour in which it will occur but rather with the preparation of the heart, which is what this book aims to address.

As the world grows ever dimmer, society becomes increasingly jaded, and worldwide protests ensue for reasons far deeper than the demonstrators themselves can even pinpoint— it is apparent that there is a universal cry of distress in this hour than can only be met by a Savior. My question for you is: Will we as the Church of Jesus Christ make a difference?

The answer begins on a personal level, which is why I believe the Lord has placed this book in your hands. I encourage you to study it carefully. Some of it is going to dig deep; some of it will run completely contrary to much of the popular theology being espoused today. Yet as you read this book, be mindful of Acts 17:11 which speaks of a certain type of believers in Christ who "were more noble than those in Thessalonica, in that they received the word with all readiness of mind, and searched the scriptures daily, whether these things were so." I challenge you to do likewise—searching the Scriptures to see if they bear witness to what is found within these pages—and see if you don't emerge gripped by truth and holding the very heart of God.

A note to my readers: As in any architectural design, it is imperative that a solid foundation first be laid before proceeding. So is the case with this book. The theoretical framework presented within the first few chapters is the very necessary foundation for the truths built upon it in subsequent chapters. Once you move past these foundational beginnings, you will find the chapters becoming increasingly personal to you as a believer in Christ. And as you press through to the end, carefully maintaining an open heart to what the Holy Spirit is speaking, something of God will come into you. You will be brought to a revelation of Christ—a depth of understanding that perhaps you are only scratching the surface of right now.

In short, this is a word from the Lord for those who desire truth, strength, and direction that conclusively promises to keep them in the coming days—to the purpose that they may be a source of blessing and hope to others. It is for those who are serious about the call of God on their life; serious about what it means to be part of the Church of Jesus Christ in these last days.

I pray this includes you.

THE

180°

SERVING
JESUS IN A
CULTURE OF
EXCESS

CHRISTIAN

The Church That
Loses Its Calling

Stand in the middle of Times Square in New York City and do a 360. I guarantee that your senses will be overloaded within seconds. You will find it nearly impossible to fully absorb the entire array of stimuli—flashing lights, theaters, souvenir shops, the aroma of Halal food wafting from the street carts, the cacophony of horns and sirens among the never-ending traffic on Broadway . . . and, of course, a man dressed in red suddenly trying to coerce you into taking a double-decker bus tour.

The scene never escapes me, for the window of my office faces the very spot where the ball drops every New Year's Eve. It is as if the Lord felt it necessary to give my eyes a snapshot and my conscience a reminder of the world of excess that we live in—one that battles incessantly for the affection of our heart . . . and, if we are not careful, wins.

While not every city has an outward display quite as outlandish as New York City does, today there is simply no escaping the underlying beckoning of the world, the enemy, and even our own flesh. It may begin as a subtle, yet insidious luring—a drawing back to old familiar comforts and pursuits, yet it eventually leads us down a pathway other than the one Christ has called us to walk. It's no wonder that many individuals and even churches, though beginning this journey by hearing from the Holy Spirit, somehow end up completely off course—some utterly unaware of just how far from the heart of God they have strayed.

Thus was the case with the Corinthian church. The believers in Corinth lost sight of the path God had called them to follow, rendering them almost entirely unable to hear what the Lord was speaking to them through the apostle Paul. The result? Powerlessness. Eventually? Loss of calling.

I fear somehow that we find ourselves in a dangerously similar situation today. In much of the Western world, we live in a society of excess that closely resembles ancient Corinth. We, too, are called to an incredible inheritance in Christ as individuals and as a strategic part of His Church. We have been left on this earth for the same purpose as they were—to be a representation of Jesus Christ to a lost generation. And yet, just like the Corinthians, many of us remain completely oblivious to the peril in which we stand.

The Lord graciously sent His Word to the Corinthian church through the apostle Paul in hopes of bringing it back to the way of truth. In the same way, I believe the Lord has a Word for us today so that we might not end up on the pathway that leads to a loss of calling. If ever there were a critical hour to hear what the Holy Spirit is speaking, it is now. We are living in a Corinthian moment, and it is imperative that we seriously reconsider what it means to be a part of the Church of Jesus Christ in these last days.

For some, that may even mean making a 180-degree turn.

The Corinthian Story

So what exactly happened to the Corinthian church? And what critical lessons does the Lord long to show us through their example?

Before I answer this, I invite you first to take a quick journey with me into Corinth—a city notorious for its wealth and indulgence. According to the *Zondervan Pictorial Encyclopedia of the Bible,* it was one of the most strategically located cities in the ancient world. Not only was Corinth the Roman capital of the province of Achaea, it was the richest port and largest city in southern Greece. This powerful commercial center easily became the meeting place for people from all over the world who journeyed there to trade and live. In fact, the height of its population consisted of approximately 700,000.[1]

Drawing such an eclectic array of nationalities and cultures, Corinth was a natural place for the pursuit of pleasure, immorality and various forms of idolatry to flourish. One of its main temples, devoted to the worship of Aphrodite, had more than 1,000 priestesses who engaged in prostitution as an act of worship.

To live as a Corinthian meant to live in luxury, an expression that has even endured to modern times as a description of profligate living. The people of this city considered themselves educated, refined, and affluent beyond most. An insatiable lust for fame, money and power continued to run rampant, just like it does in much of the world today. Every man was focused on living for the betterment of himself—not only in the society at large, but in the Church as well. Here we find the root of the Corinthian problem.

Somehow the Corinthian church had allowed the secular thinking of the surrounding society to infiltrate the church, even to the point where they wholeheartedly embraced it. Paul recognized that this errant thinking was beginning to manifest itself in ways that, if not dealt with, would ultimately cost the Corinthian church the calling of God.

A Downward Spiral

How did a small crack in their spiritual foundation widen to a chasm that required the apostle's strong rebuke? As we look at the six stages of the Corinthian church's spiritual decline, my prayer is that you would recognize this deadly spiral as it applies to your own situation and halt any one of these stages before reaching the final and most deadly one.

1. The Church Became Focused on the Elevation of Man

The apostle Paul had no choice but to deliver a grim verdict to those he had so faithfully taught:

> For you are still controlled by your sinful nature. You are jealous of one another and quarrel with each other. Doesn't that prove you are controlled by your sinful nature? Aren't you living like people of the world? When one of you says, "I am a follower of Paul," and another says, "I follow Apollos," aren't you acting just like people of the world? (1 Cor. 3:3-4, *NLT*).

It seemingly started out as legitimate spiritual preferences, but soon the church of Corinth had begun to put their focus on specific preachers and teachers, elevating them to a level that should only be given to Christ. This resulted in divisions among the Body of Christ.

Is it not the same in churches today where many attempt to elevate one preacher above another? Are we not, in many ways, as divided as the Corinthian church was? It all begins with, "So-and-so is preaching Sunday—I'll be sure to be there." It is a man-focus, and that focus is deadly.

In our churches, Jesus Christ alone must be the focal point of our thoughts and actions. We are not to simply follow other men. We are called to look beyond ourselves and other fallible human beings and become like Christ.

2. The Church Allowed Carnal and Exploitative Preachers to Lead Them

A man-focus not only resulted in divisions based on theologies and personalities, it also opened the Corinthian church to the influence of carnal and exploitative preachers. A wrong philosophy had crept in, and they began to follow men who exalted themselves rather than turning the people to Christ. Paul strongly rebuked them, saying:

> For ye suffer fools gladly, seeing ye yourselves are wise. For ye suffer, if a man bring you into bondage, if a man devour you, if a man take of you, if a man exalt himself, if a man smite you on the face (2 Cor. 11:19-20).

In other words, you have opened your heart to these fools. You have allowed them to bring you into bondage, to take from you, to make a mockery of who you are truly called to be in Christ.

Nevertheless, personal pleasure and happiness did not cease to be the Corinthians' primary objective. Because they were focused on themselves and what these preachers promised to do for them, they were unable to recognize the serious ramifications that their actions would bring to the church. They were drawn to "God's man of the hour" and "God's miracle-worker of the hour," despite the fact that these exalted ones were not operating under the anointing of God. Instead these carnal preachers were seeking their own wealth and prestige by using the church.

Don't you see this happening today? Brazen, ungodly men stand in pulpits and instruct their congregations to close their Bibles, proclaiming, "It is a new day; the Spirit of God is doing something new in our midst!" Refusing to heed Paul's rebuke and putting up with such "fools" is as dangerous as playing with the devil himself. Yet these charlatans have an advantage as naturally gifted speakers, easily able to move people into the realm of the emotions. They bring the people up to the mountain, bring them down to the valley, bring them to the point of tears and, by the end of the message, bring their hand around to everyone's wallet. It never changes.

Ultimately these preachers bring the congregation into bondage, promising them great things—how to be their best self, how to have a positive attitude to bring about health and wealth. The end result, as Paul says, is slavery to man and incorrect teaching. That is how the enemy works in the Church—he masquerades as an angel of light to deceive many into a false hope of unending happiness.

3. The Church Compromised Their Ability to Hear and Receive Truth

Paul must have felt great discouragement when he said, "And I, brethren, could not speak unto you as unto spiritual, but as unto carnal, even as unto babes in Christ. I have fed you with milk, and not with meat: for hitherto ye were not able to bear it, neither yet now are ye able" (1 Cor. 3:1-2).

As the Corinthians opened themselves to exploitative preaching, it led to an inability to hear and receive truth. Paul confirmed this, explaining that he desired to speak to them of more weighty spiritual matters, yet they were unable to bear it. Instead, he was forced to treat them as children in Christ who could only be fed with spiritual "milk." Paul wanted to provide meat for them that would enable them to weather the storms of life, but their inability to turn away from the self-seeking philosophies of these preachers shut their ears to it. Eventually, when God spoke, they could not receive it.

What else could be expected when the church's doctrine had become a smorgasbord where everyone could pick and choose what he or she wanted to hear? And all they wanted to hear was how loved, how blessed, and how powerful they were; or perhaps steps to living a stress-free life. The seemingly difficult sayings of God were easily avoided. Any personal sacrifice, suffering or giving of self and resources was bypassed in favor of a softer, less confrontational, gospel.

Sounds like much of the preaching in the Church of Jesus Christ today.

4. The Church Took on a False Spiritual Identity

You can sense Paul's frustration as he told the Corinthians, "Now ye are full, now ye are rich, ye have reigned as kings without us: and I would to God ye did reign, that we also might reign with you. For I think that God hath set forth us the apostles last, as it were appointed to death: for we are made a spectacle unto the world, and to angels, and to men. We are fools for Christ's sake, but ye are wise in Christ; we are weak, but ye are strong; ye are honourable, but we are despised" (1 Cor. 4:8-10).

Paul said in essence, "I wish you were actually reigning in Christ as the Scriptures declare. I would join you and reign with you. But as true apostles, we are appointed last, appointed to death, made a show for everyone to see. You are wise, yet we are fools for Christ. You are honorable, yet we have been called by Christ to abandon ourselves and are therefore regarded as despised by all men. You have become completely other than what we are."

Tyrannical preachers had brought them an inaccurate theology, assuring the Corinthians that they were complete; there was nothing more they needed. The people happily embraced the idea that they were rich and reigning—they were all apostles and prophets now! Yet because they believed they were strong in themselves, the power of God eluded them. Paul wrote elsewhere to the Corinthians, "When I am weak, then am I strong" (2 Cor. 12:10).

5. The Church Became Tolerant of Sinful Practices

Like a grieving father of errant children, Paul censured the sin that had been allowed to go unchecked in their midst. He wrote, "It is reported commonly that there is fornication among you, and such fornication as is not so much as named among the Gentiles, that one should have his father's wife. And ye are puffed up, and have not rather mourned, that he that hath done this deed might be taken away from among you" (1 Cor. 5:1-2).

We can learn much from the Corinthian church's lack of focus in following Paul's example and teaching. Among the lessons is how to recognize a false teacher. A carnal preacher will not challenge sin because, God forbid, some of the congregation might leave, along with their tithes. He will tell everyone—including the fornicators, adulterers and thieves—how much God loves them and that they are just fine, even though they remain unrepentant in their sins. In such churches, the blood of Christ is used as an excuse to continue illicit behaviors while confidently asserting, "God forgives me, and I won't let you condemn me."

Tolerance for sinful practices had grossly pervaded the Corinthian church. It was a tolerance for the things that separate people from God, not just in time but for eternity. This same practice of preaching only the forgiveness of God without proclaiming His holiness and our call to be like Him is evident in much of the teaching in churches around the world today. Sin is deadly; you cannot play with sin and still walk with a holy God.

6. The Church Lost Its Heart for the Poor

Paul's words to the Corinthian church about their behavior toward the poor shouts his righteous indignation over their lack of spiritual insight and compassion:

> When ye come together therefore into one place, this is not to eat the Lord's supper. For in eating every one taketh before other his own supper: and one is hungry, and another is drunken. What? have ye not houses to eat and to drink in? or despise ye the church of God, and shame them that have not? what shall I say to you? shall I praise you in this? I praise you not (1 Cor. 11:20-22).

This is the last of the six stages in the downward spiral toward a loss of calling, and it is the most telling stage of a church's true spiritual condition. The Corinthian church ended up pushing the poor and disadvantaged out of their collective consciousness. Paul must have been brokenhearted when he reminded them, "For I have received of the Lord that which also I delivered unto you, that the Lord Jesus the same night in which he was betrayed took bread: and when he had given thanks, he brake it, and said, Take, eat: this is my body, which is broken for you: this do in remembrance of me" (1 Cor. 11:23-24). He was saying, "*This* is the Christ you should be gathering around. Jesus gave His life to be broken for others, and you should be doing the same."

Where was this Christ in the Corinthian church? Self-gratification was the driving factor in the lives of many of them as they gathered around what they thought was the Lord's Table. Instead of representing Christ by following His servant example, they ignored those for whom He had given His life.

The church that loses its calling loses its heart for the poor. It is as simple as that. You cannot have a heart for the poor and be preoccupied with self at the same time. It is like trying to mix oil and water.

The Choice: Self or Christ?

How is it possible to gather at the communion table yet not have a heart for those who are dying in this world—those who are heading to a Christ-less eternity? How can we come to this table and say, "I am of Christ, and Christ is of me" if we are pushing the very work of God out of our consciousness?

What happened in the Corinthian church serves as a crucial warning for us today. If you are part of the Church yet have no problem simply going about your daily business and the pursuit of things you enjoy in life, never once taking thought to the poor and disadvantaged, something is wrong. If you can sit in front of the computer or television for hours and yet remain indifferent to the cry of the young generation all around us—those who are desperately looking for hope and help, who "faint from hunger at the head of every street" (see Lam. 2:19)— something is very wrong indeed. It is not just physical provision they need, but spiritual provision—a word from God about life; hope for tomorrow. We have been given these things in Christ, and we are meant to use them to reach out to the world around us. In fact, we as the Church today have the potential to make an incredible difference in society for those who are confused, marginalized, addicted, oppressed—all those who are wondering how they will make it until tomorrow. But will we make a difference? It all depends on whether we choose to live for ourselves or for others.

I Don't Want to Go There

Jonah is a textbook case of what happens when a person knows what God is speaking but refuses to make the choice to live for others. The Lord instructed Jonah to go to the city of Ninevah to warn the people of coming judgment. However, in his heart Jonah simply concluded, *I don't want to go there.* The natural man or woman does not want to go to a place where he or she will be spent for the needs of other people. Obedience to the call must be a work of the Spirit.

> But Jonah rose up to flee unto Tarshish from the presence of the LORD, and went down to Joppa; and he found a ship going to Tarshish: so he paid the fare thereof, and went down into it, to go with them unto Tarshish from the presence of the LORD (Jon. 1:3).

Jonah knew the basis of this commission was God's mercy, and he knew he was called to be a herald of that mercy to a wicked and undeserving people. Yet Jonah did his best to avert this pathway of a life given for the sake of others. Here we see a picture of a person who chooses to join "the church of another opinion." He is a type of man who doctrinally shops until he finds a voice that does not confront his error but rather confirms and even praises his wayward focus. Notice that the Scripture says Jonah paid the fare. You can bet that you will always pay a price to join the "church of another opinion."

What was God's response to Jonah's self-choice?

> But the LORD sent out a great wind into the sea, and there was a mighty tempest in the sea, so that the ship was like to be broken. . . . And he said unto them, Take me up, and cast me forth into the sea; so shall the sea be calm unto you: for I know that for my sake this great tempest is upon you. . . . So they took up Jonah, and cast him forth into the sea: and the sea ceased from her raging. . . . Now the LORD had prepared a great fish to swallow up Jonah. And Jonah was in the belly of the fish three days and three nights (Jon. 1:4,12-17).

Jonah was thrust into the belly of a whale . . . for three days! A hopeless situation when relying on personal strength, wouldn't you agree? Something had to happen.

> Then Jonah prayed unto the LORD his God out of the fish's belly, And said, I cried by reason of mine affliction unto the LORD, and he heard me; out of the belly of hell cried I, and thou heardest my voice. For thou

hadst cast me into the deep, in the midst of the seas; and the floods compassed me about: all thy billows and thy waves passed over me. Then I said, I am cast out of thy sight; yet I will look again toward thy holy temple. The waters compassed me about, even to the soul: the depth closed me round about, the weeds were wrapped about my head (Jon. 2:1-5).

The word "weeds" is not only translated as weeds in the Hebrew, but it is also the word used for the Red Sea—the symbol of an impossible place of no escape without supernatural help. Jonah was saying, "Oh, God, the things I thought were going to make me happy, the things I thought were going to bring me into freedom, it is as if they are wrapped around my head and they are laughing at me. Now I have been brought into a trial, and without Your strength, there is no way I can get out!"

Now I want you to consider for a moment a possible reason for the trial or inner distress you may be facing today. Could it simply be because there is something in you that does not want to fully obey God? In your heart you are thinking, "This was supposed to be about me. I came to God in my bondage and struggle, and He was going to make me into something great. But now He is calling me to be poured out? I don't want to go there!"

However, just as the Lord delivered Jonah, I am confident that He is going to deliver the true believer from the error of this generation. How, you ask?

In God's mercy, a great trial is coming! The false believer will not be delivered, but the true believer will be saved from error by this great trial—a trial we will not be able to figure out or escape from in our own strength. Perhaps you are already in the midst of a great personal trial now. But you must remember that behind the scenes, God is moving you to something He has prepared for you.

Once Jonah finally came to the point of obedience, the fish vomited him out on dry land. That was the key—deliverance came when he agreed with God, saying, "I will obey You. What You called me to do, I will do." His focus was finally off himself.

It is no different for us today. Every Christian is called to live not for himself or for herself, but for other people, beginning with the most disadvantaged. This was the call on the Corinthian church, and it is our call today. Of course we all fight against self-focus and tendencies toward self-preservation. We have an inherent sinful nature that just wants to live for self and enjoy a comfortable life. Oh, we wouldn't mind having a few nice exploits for God here and there, but everything in our fallen human nature absolutely resists this idea of living a life that is entirely spent for the things of God. We are all the same in this way, and that is why we must come to the throne of God, acknowledging our lack of desire and strength to continually reach out to others. We must say, "Lord, you have the resources of life that I need. I ask You to give me the heart and strength to do all that You have called me to do."

God will surely answer that cry. After all, it is all about redeeming souls for the sake of His kingdom. This is where the true life of Christ is found.

Note

1. Merrill C. Tenney, ed., *The Zondervan Pictorial Encyclopedia of the Bible,* 5 vols. (Grand Rapids, MI: Zondervan, 1975), vol. 1, pp. 960-964.

Embracing the Cross

The apostle Paul lived in Corinth for nearly a year and a half, so we can be rightly assured of at least a few things: The Corinthian church heard the message of the cross. They knew Christ died and rose again on the third day. They were aware that they had access to power that would enable them to triumph over every enemy. They knew they had been promised a new heart, mind and spirit. No doubt many of them gladly accepted all of these things that Paul shared. After all, the Corinthians, like all people, lived with an incredible depth of need in their hearts; a hunger for truth.

So how then did this church that Paul founded on one of his missionary journeys end up to be inarguably the most difficult church he ever had to pastor? Simply put, they were willing to embrace the cross as the answer to their personal need for salvation, yet unwilling to embrace the call to follow Christ as Lord. They took the salvation but ultimately lived for self.

It is likely that this self-choice was at least partly fueled by their impression of what life would look like should they choose to fully embrace the cross. I dare say they might sum it up in one word: foolishness. Paul said it this way:

> For the preaching of the cross is to them that perish foolishness; but unto us which are saved it is the power of God (1 Cor. 1:18).

It is important to recognize that God calls His people not only to embrace the cross as the sufficiency of the atonement—but to also embrace the deeper implication of what this walk with Christ really means. In Matthew 16:24, Jesus said, "If anyone desires to come after me, let him deny himself, and take up his cross, and follow me." The Son of God left heaven and came to earth as a man to go to a cross— a Roman instrument of execution—and pour out His life to provide our forgiveness and redemption. He gave Himself as a sacrifice for many, and He calls His followers to walk a similar path. This is the part of the cross that the Corinthian church refused to embrace. Not surprisingly, for the idea of giving of oneself for the sake of others is utter foolishness to those who are pursuing a pathway leading to spiritual death.

We as the Church face this same dilemma today, particularly in the Western world. We have a tendency to embrace only one side of the cross—forgiveness of sin and the peace that comes from knowing God. Of course the Lord does freely offer these things. For those who are living in captivity or those who are dealing with an ever-increasing sense of hopelessness in their heart, the cross of Christ is the answer. However, while we as humans tend to want the assurance of a sound and solid future in heaven, many of us are not willing to go any deeper. It is another example of self-focus versus Christ-focus. *I take what I need and ignore the rest.*

If only we could grasp the truth that Paul was trying to reveal to the Corinthian church: It is not the way of the cross that is foolishness. In reality, it is this philosophy of "every man for himself" that will ultimately prove to be both foolish and powerless.

Of course it would be unfair to single out the Corinthians as the only people who chose the self-serving life rather than the self-sacrificing path of the cross. In fact, we see the fallout of this self-choice time after time throughout the Scriptures, beginning at . . . well, the beginning.

Adam and Eve

Adam and Eve, the first people of God, walked in a right relationship with Him. Their intimacy with God was their covering, and all their needs were addressed. No shame, no guilt—just God. Satan knew he had to get hold of this perfection somehow; he had to pervert the thinking of these two who were called to be co-laborers with God.

When Satan came to Eve in the Garden, he approached her with his own dark wisdom. In direct conflict with God's words, Satan persuaded Eve to believe that she could chart her own course independently of what God had spoken.

Yea, hath God said, Ye shall not eat of every tree of the garden? And the serpent said unto the woman, Ye shall not surely die: For God doth know that in the day ye eat thereof, then your eyes shall be opened, and ye shall be as gods, knowing good and evil (Gen. 3:1,4-5).

Satan said to Eve, "If you do it my way, it will satisfy the deepest inner need in your life. You do not have to listen to what God says. God's ways are too narrow. There is a bigger way, another way to arrive at what you are looking for. Chart your own course; determine your own destiny! The journey will be pleasant to your eyes and will make you wise. Just do it my way!"

Both Eve and her husband succumbed to the lie, partaking of what God clearly told them not to touch. What happened next?

> And the eyes of them both were opened, and they knew that they were naked; and they sewed fig leaves together, and made themselves aprons (Gen. 3:7).

How often does the devil succeed with this very same tactic today? Remember, the devil is the king of darkness—the prince of this world. His goal is to get people to look away from the cross of Christ. He convinces them that the narrow pathway that Christ has prescribed is foolishness. "Why should you have to live a life that is so restricted? Why not enjoy at least some of what the world has to offer? After all, you don't want to be completely out of touch with this generation." And so he lures them to what appears to be a more pleasant and less difficult option, promising that they will become wise along the way. Little do they know that the end of this path is a loss of the covering of God.

That is exactly what happened to Adam and Eve. Satan led them into spiritual and moral bankruptcy, and they no longer had any power to stand against their enemy. When the glory of God was their covering, the devil could not touch them. But the moment they bit into Satan's logic, they were forced to make coverings for themselves, as ridiculous as that fig-leaf clothing was.

Similarly, when you and I are no longer walking in God's way, we must resort to our own wisdom in attempts to figure out how to win the battle. We begin cultivating devices out of our natural minds—creating our own coverings, battle strategies, steps to take, pathways to what we perceive to be victory. We end up exchanging what we considered the "foolishness" of the way of the cross only to live in the folly of human wisdom.

Not Exactly What I Had in Mind

What is it about the human condition that causes us to lose focus on God's call? Why was Satan able to tempt Adam and Eve, successfully luring them away from the plan God gave them that would have lead them to nothing but His glory? Why do we have such difficulty fully embracing the cross?

Herein lies the problem: Our focus is so deeply ingrained in worldly goals, worldly standards and self-centeredness that we are completely unattracted to where the cross will lead us. We say to ourselves, *If this is God, there is nothing in it for me. How is this going to give me the fine robes and the best seat at the banquets? How is this going to bring me to a place where people will call me "teacher, teacher" in the public sphere? How is this going to get me closer access to power and the other things I am looking for in life?*

It is evident that the truths Paul taught the Corinthian church did not quite fit their vision of what they believed should be garnered from an association with the church. So they began to challenge the authority of Scripture, and they challenged it simply based on the image of Paul. Men stood in pulpits declaring, "Yes, we agree his letters are weighty, but his bodily presence is contemptible, and his speech lacks the eloquence and the wisdom that we are able to bring to you" (see 2 Cor. 10:10). They essentially told the people, "This following of Christ . . . when you look at Paul, is this what you want to look like? Is this what you want to be? This Paul who is nothing more than a vagabond traveling from church to church, working with his own hands, making tents to supply his own needs . . . is that what you want your life to amount to?"

Scripture further underscores the human predilection for moving away from God's call in its description of Jesus Christ and the way of the cross:

> For he shall grow up before him as a tender plant, and as a root out of a dry ground: he hath no form nor comeliness; and when we shall see him, there is no beauty that we should desire him. He is despised and rejected of men; a man of sorrows, and acquainted with grief: and we hid as it were our faces from him; he was despised, and we esteemed him not (Isa. 53:2-3).

We "esteemed Him not" means that we looked at Him— we made a judgment in our hearts, concluding, "This does not make a very good picture. This is not what I want my life to be. I don't want to be ordinary. I don't want to give my all to the needs of others. I don't want to walk on the side of being misunderstood and have to endure persecution everywhere I go."

Called in Weakness

I cannot help but wonder if much has changed in our generation. If the apostle Paul were in our midst today, would people flock to him like they do to the polished and eloquent? After all, not only did Paul come in "fear and trembling," he wasn't even handsome!

In the Western world, we, like the Corinthian church, have placed a great emphasis on education, prestige and appearance. But this is not the litmus test for how God chooses people to represent Himself and His kingdom. He chooses men and women who are seemingly of no value in the world's eyes to show His awesome power.

> For ye see your calling, brethren, how that not many wise men after the flesh, not many mighty, not many noble, are called: But God hath chosen the foolish things of the world to confound the wise; and God hath chosen the weak things of the world to confound the things which are mighty; and base things of the world, and things which are despised, hath God chosen, yea, and things which are not, to bring to nought things that are (1 Cor. 1:26-28).

It is hard for the natural man to lay hold of this concept since so much of the church has been indoctrinated with self-centered theology. Those who are rich and powerful have become the church's examples. We gravitate toward teaching that exalts the wise and the mighty of this world, but ultimately, these are the same people who oppress and marginalize the uneducated and the poor. God will confound this kind of wisdom by selecting those who are deemed "unfit" by society to instruct us in His goodness and grace. He does this so that He alone may receive the glory and that we will be convinced that all power comes from Him and not ourselves (see 1 Cor. 1:26-31).

God has called us to something far greater, something that is way beyond ourselves. He does not want our strength or our wisdom. He has not called us to figure it all out, for the wisdom of this world is foolishness to God. We need to refocus on the truth that our human effort—our qualifications and abilities—is irrelevant in God's eyes. His power is made perfect in our weakness (see 2 Cor. 12:9).

What He is looking for is the one who comes to the throne of God and says, "I am nothing. I have no strength or power. Without Your strength, I cannot pray, preach or live as a Christian." This is the very one who will know the touch of God. In fact, I know of such a person.

Not many would leave their job as a pharmacist in order to become a furniture salesman, yet that is exactly what a certain gentleman did as he left his position in Colombia and arrived in New York. He immediately found a church in the city and began volunteering by translating sermons from English into Spanish. Little did he know that this simple post would become his Bible school over the next seven years. By his own admission, he was utterly changed by the Word of God through this process, and something amazing began to happen. He received an anointing from God and began to actively participate in the sermons—before the preacher spoke a line, the young man was receiving the same word!

One day he came across a huge world map that had been set up in the foyer of his church. Congregants were challenged to place a colored pin in a country of their choice and commit to praying for it. Pushing a tiny pin into Spain, he went forth and began to pray fervently from that day on. Not long afterwards, he felt God was calling him to step out in faith and go to Spain.

He could not help but wonder at the time—*How am I going to go? I don't have any support or savings, nor a single theological degree under my belt.* Despite these questions, deep down he was convinced that if God were calling him, He would make a way. The man shared his heart with a leader at the church, and within a week, one miracle after another occurred. In no time at all he had received a full year of support from a number of anonymous sources!

So off he headed to Spain in submission to the Lord. Upon arrival, he met with the leader of one of the major denominations in the country and announced, "Here I am. I am not a Bible school graduate, but God has called me here."

This denominational leader looked at him and said, "Well, we do not have a place for you here. But none of our ministers will go into Northern Africa to witness to the Islamic population there. We cannot find anyone willing."

What do you think that man's reply was?

He simply said, "I will go."

Now, three years later, he pastors a church of approximately 140 believers in Northern Africa. He has learned to speak three different languages, as his congregation is made up of three different people groups—predominantly Muslims who have converted to following Christ. And what exactly does he do? Well, he does what he has always done—he simply stands up and trusts the Lord. In return, God anoints him for the work he has been called to.

"I have never been happier in my whole life," he told me.

Since then, this man has been widely recognized and officially credentialed. But what most people do not realize is that God had already "credentialed" him long before man did!

This true story clearly demonstrates the calling and the power of God. Here was a man who had never taken a cultural course on reaching the African Muslim, did not know much of the language and had no official ministry training whatsoever. Yet he got the message—God does not call us in our own strength, but in our weakness.

Responding to the Lord's call does not require you to evaluate your gifts and skills before you act. If it is the Holy Spirit's leading, He will give you the burden for a certain group of people or country and then lead you from there. Remember, God is not looking for worldly wisdom. He is looking for a simple willingness to embrace the cross—foolishness to those who are perishing, but to us, the power of God to do all He has called us to do.

When the Way Is Forsaken

As we have seen, there are many people who just cannot accept this idea of being called in weakness, who do not like the image of a life in which the cross is fully embraced. But what about the picture of a life where the way of the cross of Christ is rejected? Consider the parable Jesus told in the book of Matthew:

> But when the unclean spirit is gone out of a man, he walketh through dry places, seeking rest, and findeth none (Matt. 12:43).

This is a type of people who have received Christ, or a form of Christ at least. Perhaps they received Him as Savior yet remain unwilling to walk with Him as their Lord. As a result, their life is marked by emptiness. They may sing nice songs on Sunday morning, but inside is spiritual bankruptcy—nothing of God's light is pouring through them into the society around them. So they start down a pathway of selfishness—an empty pathway that never satisfies. This is exactly what happens in the following verses:

> Then he saith, I will return into my house from whence I came out; and when he is come, he findeth it empty, swept, and garnished. Then goeth he, and taketh with himself seven other spirits more wicked than himself, and they enter in and dwell there: and the last state of that man is worse than the first. Even so shall it be also unto this wicked generation (Matt. 12:44-45).

It is amazing when you consider the significance of the number "seven" in the Bible. God created the world in six days, and on the seventh day He rested. The book of Proverbs speaks of the seven pillars with which Wisdom builds her house. There are seven churches in the book of Revelation. If you were to thoroughly study the "sevens" throughout the Bible, you will see that this number symbolizes the perfection and rest of God.

However, when we reject the way of Christ, there is another pathway, another "seven" with an equally powerful significance. The Scripture says that the original unclean spirit takes seven spirits that are even more wicked than himself, and they all end up indwelling that man. In other words, whatever that man once was comes back to him again, this time in manifold power, and he ends up in a condition far worse than when he began.

The Life of Christ in You

On the other hand, there is a fullness in Christ that awaits those who do not forsake the way of the cross—those who take that step of surrender and truly say, "Lord, I am giving You my life." I remember when I first accepted Christ as my Savior. It was actually not until about two years later that I one day turned to my wife and said, "I want the whole thing or nothing at all. I want everything that Christ is calling me to, or I don't want any part of it." The Lord knew I meant it, and from that day forward He began to open my heart in a new way and lead me in the direction of His heart.

So what will happen as you choose to fully embrace the life and cross of Christ? Paul spoke these words:

But of him are ye in Christ Jesus, who of God is made unto us wisdom, and righteousness, and sanctification, and redemption (1 Cor. 1:30).

First, you embrace His power. It is not just a mental agreement with the fact that a Savior died on Calvary; it is receiving the power of God in exchange for your weakness.

You find wisdom. It is the wisdom of God, not the wisdom of this world. The Lord opens your understanding, and you will not be found among those who are "ever learning and never able to come to the knowledge of the truth" (2 Tim. 3:7). You hear Him saying, "This is the way, walk ye in it."

You find His righteousness. When you walk selflessly in Him, you gain the knowledge that there is no longer any condemnation. You realize that the devil has no right to you because the covering of God that was lost in the Garden is now yours again through Christ Jesus. Your frailty and your failings are covered. The Father looks at you and sees you through the covering of Jesus—He sees you as righteous as His own Son.

You find your sanctification. In other words, God grants you victory over temptation and besetting sin. As you walk in this power, you will know what it is to be daily conformed into His image.

You find the full power and freedom of your redemption. The moment you begin to move in the direction of God's heart, you experience His life flowing through you. The old things that used to limit you lose their hold, and you begin to experience the fullness of your new life in Christ.

As you continue to follow the pathway of the cross, God will lead you to be kind to the unthankful, to help those in need, and to be a hand stretched out in His name and with His power. Your mind will begin to be transformed from the thinking of this world, and you will walk in a newfound liberty.

Now embracing the cross might just start in your marriage or with your children. It might start with your friends . . .

or your enemies. It might start in your workplace, on your street or in your community. But it definitely starts with the prayer, "God Almighty, to the death, I am yours. If I have to go to jail, if I have to die, I am yours. If I have to forfeit everything I thought would make me happy . . . if I have to give up the future I dreamed I would have—I give it to you, Lord. You are my Savior *and* Lord. I choose *both* sides of the cross."

Be Sure Your Sin Will Find You Out

"Be sure your sin will find you out" (Num. 32:23). It is quite a familiar verse indeed—whether it triggers sudden flashbacks of an encounter with an angry preacher, or it is the Scripture that you use to caution your children when they are on the brink of making a bad decision. In any event, this verse is typically spoken as a word of warning to someone who has something hidden in the closet that he or she is trying to keep there. However, when you read it within its context, the verse has quite a different application—particularly in light of what we have been learning thus far from the example of the Corinthian church.

> And Moses said unto them, If ye will do this thing, if ye will go armed before the LORD to war, and will go all of you armed over Jordan before the LORD, until he hath driven out his enemies from before him, and the land be subdued before the LORD: then afterward ye shall return, and be guiltless before the LORD, and before Israel; and this land shall be your possession before the LORD. But if ye will not do so, behold, ye have sinned against the LORD: and be sure your sin will find you out (Num. 32:20-23).

Here we find Moses speaking to the Children of Israel, reviewing God's plan for driving out their enemies and entering the Promised Land. At this point, some of the Israelite tribes had already received what they felt to be their inheritance. However, there were other tribes, brothers and sisters in Christ, who had not yet gone into the Promised Land to claim what was rightfully theirs. It was understood that those who had found what they were looking for would not settle in until all the others had received their inheritance as well.

The Lord, speaking through Moses, was actually issuing a strict warning to the Children of Israel: "If you settle in and focus on yourselves to the exclusion of all others; if you let your brothers struggle to gain their inheritance and, in some cases, perhaps even be defeated in claiming that which has been promised to them, you can be sure that this sin will find you out."

Wasn't this the very attitude that was at the root of the problem in Corinth? No wonder Paul wept countless tears over this church. He even traveled back to see them three times and wrote to them, "I love you—I am fighting for you to present you as a pure bride to Christ" (see 2 Cor. 11:2). Paul knew that their theological focus was wrong and that there would surely be a price to pay. Unfortunately, it is evident from those who have studied the Corinthian situation that the problems continued to persist even after some of Paul's most impassioned pleas. Most likely there were still many who failed to heed his warnings even after his death.

Bearing this in mind, we would be wise to heed any words of warning that the Lord has lovingly left His children with today. Consider, for example, the following passage in Proverbs:

If thou forbear to deliver them that are drawn unto death, and those that are ready to be slain; if thou sayest, Behold, we knew it not; doth not he that pondereth the

t consider it? And he that keepeth thy soul,
h not he know it? And shall not he render to
ery man according to his works? (Prov. 24:11-12).

Here is what the Lord was saying: If you forbear (that
is, draw back) from delivering those in peril, if you knew or
at least remotely considered the calling of Christ on your
life, yet you still conclude, "No, I don't want this. I don't
want to go this second mile for the sake of others"—or if
you hold back from doing good under the guise of, "I
didn't know"—shall God not render to every man according to his works?

Many people today choose to live in darkness rather
than allowing themselves to be confronted by the truth of
God. But one day they will each stand before the throne of
God and be required to explain their lack of care for others.
"Well, I didn't know. If I had known, I would have gone."
Yet I believe every man and woman who has ever sat with a
Bible in his or her hands is without excuse before the
throne of God. As Moses warned, if you do not go and fight
for your brother, if you just sit here and build your own
house and concern yourself with your own life, be sure your
sin will find you out. There will be a cost to you.

This sin of seeking self will always be accompanied by
an indifference to the struggle of others. What cost will
this bring to the professing church of Jesus Christ? What
will we have to deal with if we continue seeking only our
own satisfaction?

A Harvest of Corruption

There is a simple yet immutable sowing and reaping law in the kingdom of God: Whatever you plant is what you will eventually harvest. Consider Paul's explanation in the book of Galatians:

Do not be deceived, God is not mocked; for whatever a man sows, that he will also reap. For he who sows to his flesh will of the flesh reap corruption, but he who sows to the Spirit will of the Spirit reap everlasting life (Gal. 6:7-8, *NKJV*).

He who sows to his flesh—or in other words, he who sows to satisfy himself—will reap corruption. Keep in mind that this chapter of Galatians is written in the context of restoring those who have fallen. It speaks of bearing one another's burdens, doing good to all men—particularly those who are of the household of faith, going to those who have fallen and bringing them back to the knowledge of Christ. We are called to do good even to the unthankful and unholy, just as our Father in heaven does.

However, when we choose instead to plant solely to ourselves and for our own benefit, it is inevitable that we will reap corruption. We already saw this outcome as corrupt leadership eventually infiltrated the Corinthian church.

Good Times Voices in Bad Times

Evidence of the self-seeking church clearly existed elsewhere besides Corinth, offering us further warning of the repercussions of this sin. In the Book of Jeremiah, we see Israel—the people of God—in a season when judgment was at the door. Yet look at what was happening in the house of God:

> As a cage is full of birds, so are their houses full of deceit: therefore they are become great, and waxen rich. They are waxen fat, they shine: yea, they overpass the deeds of the wicked: they judge not the cause, the cause of the fatherless, yet they prosper; and the right of the needy do they not judge (Jer. 5:27-28).

These spiritual leaders were no longer challenging sinners in the house of God, no longer addressing the core issue of what separates man from God. They did not have a heart for the fatherless, made no mention of the poor, and certainly did not move the people in the direction of human need.

> Shall I not visit for these things? saith the LORD: shall not my soul be avenged on such a nation as this? A wonderful and horrible thing is committed in the land; the prophets prophesy falsely, and the priests bear rule by their means; and my people love to have it so: and what will ye do in the end thereof? (Jer. 5:29-31).

In other words, "This is a terrible thing—it is beyond thinking. The prophets are not standing and speaking for God, but instead they are full of themselves and are leading in the flesh. The prophets are speaking a message of comfort to a people who are about to go into disaster. They are not warning the people of the days ahead; they are not dealing with the issues of the heart. They rule by their own power, and everything has become a strategy now."

Doesn't this sound familiar? Preachers are speaking comfort to people who are on the brink of judgment. Nobody is talking about leaning on God, going into the prayer closet, finding out what God is saying in this hour and moving in the anointing of the Holy Spirit. Even sermons have become the product of an Internet search rather than a true seeking of God's heart and mind. It is all dominated by the natural man with his plans and strategies. *How do we reach the community? What kind of survey are we going to come up with next to get people into the house of God?*

And Jeremiah asks, "But what will you do when the end comes?"

What *will* you do?

When the Twin Towers were struck on 9/11, we had a taste of the panic—of what the Bible says is going to come to the whole world in a moment of time. Of course we do not know if the end will happen in our generation, but what if it does? What if all hell breaks out in our lifetime? Where will all the prophets of success and prosperity be then?

Jeremiah said, in effect, "You love to have it this way—a gospel that just focuses on building you up and making you feel good. You walk out feeling like you are a king, like you are ruling and reigning with Christ, whether or not you actually are. But what will happen when the end comes? What will happen if you have not really been in the Scriptures, if you have not really been walking with God?"

Perilous Days Ahead

The apostle Peter also spoke about the last days and these same voices that will emerge once again—voices that do not know God. It is always a sign of impending judgment when you see the good-time prophets arise, and that is your cue to dig into the Word of God like you never have before.

They will be mesmerizing speakers, but they will never deal with anything of the cross or what it really means to be part of the Bride of Jesus Christ. Here is what Peter said to the New Testament Church (which includes us):

> But there were false prophets also among the people, even as there shall be false teachers among you, who privily shall bring in damnable heresies, even deny-ing the Lord that bought them, and bring upon themselves swift destruction (2 Pet. 2:1).

When Peter says, "denying the Lord who bought them," it means these false prophets will deny the lordship of Christ over the believer and His right to use our lives as He sees fit. These false prophets will deny the authority of Christ, the fact that we are bought with the price of His own blood. They will deny that we are not our own anymore but instead we are to glorify God with our bodies and with our spirits. They will deny that we are called, as the Scripture says, to give our lives as a living sacrifice for God, which is our reasonable service (see Rom. 12:1). And they will deny the Lord His right of ownership over His Church.

> For when they speak great swelling words of vanity, they allure through the lusts of the flesh, through much wantonness, those that were clean escaped from them who live in error. While they promise them liberty, they themselves are the servants of corruption: for of whom a man is overcome, of the same is he brought in bondage. For if after they have escaped the pollutions of the world through the knowledge of the Lord and Saviour Jesus Christ, they are again entangled therein, and overcome, the latter end is worse with them than the beginning. For it had been better for them not to have known the way of righteousness, than, after they have known it, to turn from the holy commandment delivered unto them (2 Pet. 2:18-21).

It is through unsurrendered personal lusts that these puppeteers will succeed in drawing the people back into what they had once left behind. Many will be ensnared with the erroneous thinking that satisfaction in the Christian life comes from the things of this world. Peter said it would have been better for them not to have known the truth than to turn from the holy commandment. "Holy" means "separation from the earth's defilement," and "commandment" means "the whole moral law of God." The whole moral law of God requires us to be separate from the thinking of this world.

Remember that Peter was present when Jesus said to His disciples, "A new commandment I give unto you, that ye love one another; as I have loved you, that ye also love one another. By this shall all men know that ye are my disciples, if ye have love one to another" (John 13:34-35). This is a holy commandment! If Peter were physically with us today, he might say to us, "I was there, I saw Him when He sat at the table. We knew there were Ten Commandments, but now God in the flesh, the One who created the universe, said, 'I give you a new commandment'—it is really the eleventh commandment. Jesus said to us, 'I am calling you now to love one another as I have loved you.'"

Tragically, not only have we adopted a false concept of Christianity that has strayed far from this holy commandment, we have exported it to the far reaches of the world, completely forsaking the love and compassion for our neighbor that Jesus requires. I have been in Africa where the poor and fatherless come into the house of God without even shoes to wear, only to find preachers who have brought their false theology from the United States. These preachers rip off the poor and the fatherless, taking every last cent they have in their pocket. How long will it be before God judges this self-seeking, self-indulgent, loathsome focus in the house of God—using Jesus Christ for our own advantage? Peter said, "This is not the gospel," and Paul pleaded with the Corinthian church over the same issue.

Evicting the Corinthian Attitude in Today's Church

Be sure, Moses said, your sin will find you out. What can we do today to heed this grave warning?

Do Not Get Comfortable with Sin in the Church

The Corinthian church eventually came to a point where there was open and unconfessed sin among the people, all of which was largely met with nonchalance. It had become an atmosphere of fornication, incest, divisions and brother taking brother to court over trivial matters. However, as long as none of these things affected their own livelihood, nobody really cared. They were completely oblivious to the fact that whatever is allowed in the house of God that is an abomination to Christ ultimately affects everyone in the church.

Paul did not tell the Corinthians to disassociate from every fornicator and liar and thief, for they would have had to leave the world. But he did tell them not to eat with a brother who confessed Christ and at the same time was a fornicator, unwilling to turn from his sin. If a man willfully participates in thievery, willfully lies, willfully covets, willfully mocks God, then the church is not to associate with him. The willful sinner is different than the one who struggles. The willful sinner should never become comfortable in the church of Jesus Christ.

Do Not Rob from God

There is a related principle found in Malachi 3:8. God said to the people through the prophet Malachi, "You have robbed Me." And the people asked, "How have we robbed You? What have we done? As far as we know, we are coming to the temple." The Lord uses the illustration of tithes and offerings, but there is a deeper principle here. God was essentially telling the people, "You have robbed Me in failing to surrender to Me what I asked of you. You have changed the requirements for attending My house. You have changed the requirements for coming in and calling yourself by My name."

We find a very similar situation in our generation—the requirements have been changed. Many churches have completely eliminated the cross from their theology. They have taken out from their hymnbooks the shed blood that takes away sin. They have changed the requirement for coming in to God's house—they have robbed Him.

What I believe grieves God most is that we have robbed Him of our hearts. It is as if He would say to us, "You have robbed Me of the full heart of surrender that I was looking for that would have allowed Me to fill you from the crown of your head to the soles of your feet. If only you would have turned to Me! I would have caused you to live such a profound life that you would have stood out as a light shining in a darkened world" (see Ps. 81:13-14; Matt. 5:14; Luke 13:34).

Do Not Ascribe God's Voice to Man's Confusion

Not only was the Corinthian church tolerant of sin, they were also noted for their confusion. First Corinthians 14 says that they were using spiritual gifts for self-glory, and the end result was disorder. Think about it. If you and I could go back in history and walk into a Corinthian church service, everybody would be speaking in tongues at the same time. So-called prophets would be trying to prophesy over the top of one another. Can you imagine? Chaos and disorder everywhere.

When Paul heard these things, he told the church that people coming in would conclude they were mad! Paul said, "I would rather speak five words with my understanding, that I may teach others also, than ten thousand words in a tongue" (1 Cor. 14:19, *NKJV*). He reminded the Corinthians that they were not to use the giftings for themselves but rather for the purpose of edifying others.

For the past 15 or so years, the Western world has experienced what was supposed to be a charismatic revival. I want to suggest that it has been a Corinthian moment—nothing but confusion. People have been flying all over the world, saying, "What is in it for me? I want one more touch for myself. I want one more thing, one more gift! More for me!" The unsaved have looked at it and concluded, "These people are crazy."

Confusion is the result of self-exaltation. It is a simple principle: Hey, look at me! Look at me to the exclusion of the outsider, to the exclusion of the man or woman who is coming in and looking for God, looking for help, looking for hope. The end result is just a hodgepodge of spiritual nonsense.

We must remember that "God is not the author of confusion, but of peace" (1 Cor. 14:33). The moment in our hearts that we use what we have for others, the confusion dissipates and divine order comes into the house of God.

From Chaos to Calm

So many believers today remain confused and have trouble hearing the voice of God. It is typically due to the fact that they are merely looking to confirm the direction of their own flesh, and all the while they are holding back something that God has specifically asked them to lay down. God wants something deeper from us—He wants us to walk where He walks, to do what He does, to see people through His eyes. He wants our hands to become His hands and our voice to speak His heart. That is when He can give us a life that we can only dream about. But first we must let go of whatever we are holding on to so tightly.

I once knew a young lady who came to Christ and was so alive in God; an extraordinary worshipper in fact. She also happened to be part of one of the Broadway shows in New York City. One Sunday she came to me and said, "It can't be that God is asking me to give this up. I have lived my whole life for this career!" She was waiting for me to reassure her that it couldn't be God.

I simply replied, "Well, I don't know what the Holy Spirit is asking of you, but all I can tell you is that when God speaks to you, you should obey Him. Something greater for your life awaits you—far greater than what you think your life should be."

Aware of this struggle, I watched her over the next few weeks. I noticed her sitting closer and closer to the back of the church each service. She did come back to see me again three times or so, each time shaking her head, concluding,